And Another Thing

poems

Irene Willis

AND ANOTHER THING

POEMS

Irene Willis

International Psychoanalytic Books (IPBooks)
New York • www.IPBooks.net

in memory of my husband, Bernard Daves Rossell

This is how I honor
My mother, my father.
This is how
I sing to them.

Contents

I

II

III

IV

V

VI
Tomfoolery

I

What I Learned

This is what
I learned from them
and must have learned apace:
from my mother, vanity;
from my father, surely–grace.

Tornado Watch

I don't mean to make light of this
but when the first warning came
after that piercing signal
I deliberated, before going down
into my basement tornado room
about what I should wear.
Maybe it was akin to my mother's bit
about not being found in an accident
with safety pins–or was it something
more–like not flying through the sky
on your rooftop in an old bathrobe–
and so threw choice after choice
on the bed until I found a top and pants
that looked tornado-respectable,
washed my face, put on lipstick,
and brushed my hair before
descending with my book, flashlight,
blanket, bottled water, radio and chair.

Who Was I?

A girl. A human. That
was all I really knew.
But there in my New York
Manhattan was a country,
the block, a province.
In the street outside
the population
of the under-five-feet
would congregate,
would mill.
One had a ball,
another a rope,
someone else
a piece of chalk.
We'd jump and throw;
We'd scrawl.
Admirers of expertise,
we had our specialties:
Potsy Champ, Jumper
of Double Dutch.
In each new neighborhood
I learned again: make them
laugh or listen
and I was in.

Yes

In our home, books in glass cases.
In my grandparents' too. Good books.
Behind glass. Complete sets of Thackeray,
DeMaupassant, delightful as marzipan.
So when I found a man
With complete sets of Sir Walter Scott,
buckram-bound Dickens, a well-marked
Bullfinch, Roget's—all that—
plus a Royal portable in a gray case,
Tweed jacket with elbow patches, pipe
(and not just any pipe, a genuine meerschaum),
Everything in me shook and jelled,
Shimmered, shouted, *I will! I do!*

First Marriage

His mother was amazed
at how much his writing
had improved
since he married me.

My job was to help him—
to be his "helpmeet"—
as they might have put it.
Why not?
I tried to talk about it
but it was out of their ken—

No ken they understood
or accepted.

No kin of mine, my grandmother said
shaking me up like a kaleidoscope
and when the pieces shook out
into a different design
I reminded him—my "ex" (a term I
hate and never use but now seems right)
he didn't remember the event at all.

What good does it do to forgive
if what you're forgiving
never happened?

Is even remorse
in the eye of the beholder?

Men Who Call Their Wives "Mommy"

They met at a doctors' dance.
She thought she would get a doctor,
but she didn't.
He thought he would get a nice
WASP college girl he could take
to meet his mother, but he didn't.
Instead, he got my mother–
a cute Jewish girl
who looked like Betty Boop,
so he called her that
and she took his name.
Did he call her Mommy
before I was born? I wonder.
But she was certainly Mommy
after that.
We all called her Mommy
and that's what she was
for the rest of her life.

It started back when cigarettes
bore lipsticks' traces
and all the rooms they partied in
or sat or ate in
or slept in
turned blue, blue, blue
which meant they knew
what life was all about

the secrets of this life
where smoke was sex
and sex was smoke
and a cigarette on the nightstand
was all you had to see
because without that cigarette
it wasn't over
and without that cigarette
it might not even start.

When I met the man I married
I was seventeen–a co-ed
and he was twenty-five, in college
on the G.I. Bill.
He smoked a pipe
thoughtfully
and sucked on cigars,
turning them around and
around in his mouth
so I thought he was brilliant.
Long before the baby came
he called me Mommy.
because, he said, you're
the kind of mother
I always wanted.
Oh God! Oh Freud!

Even at seventeen, I *knew.*
The wisdom must have come
when I lit up
my first Pall Mall

I look at them now,
these guys smoking
with their eyes half-closed
out on the riverbank
or outside the building
where they work
and I watch them drawing in the smoke,
letting it out, looking as if
they're really thinking hard
and I wonder what about
and who and where and why
and do their wives and girlfriends know
and did they fall in love with that
the way I must have
the way I almost do
even now.

Daddy, blow a smoke ring,
oh please do.
I almost put my finger out
to slide it through.

My Mother's Words

Slipped him a Mickey.
Garnishee…

Why did I need to know
words like those at six

when I wanted to play,
jump rope

strap on my skates
and roll away?

Why did she need
to tell me?

Who and what
was I supposed to be?

And why did I always
fail at that?

What did my baby
brother do

except nurse, make
smelly diapers

suck his thumb
grow up to be

a big thirteen
and scratch her back?

The Cat's Mother

Who's she–the cat's mother?
my mother would say
when I spoke her
rightful pronoun, talking
to my brother or my father.

Cat's mother, hi-ho's nest,
Wreck of the Hesperus
peppered her speech, floated
in balloons over our heads
and filled my dreams.

She, the cat's mother;
our apartment the hi-ho's nest
and she, before she got dressed
in the morning or combed her hair,
The Wreck, of course, of the Hesperus.

I was the mynah bird, wondering
what the cat's mother wanted me
to say. Was it *mother, mother,*
mother, like the tick-tock stutter
of our big old clock?

Organic

When my child was three
and still in a high chair
at our kitchen table,
bib tied innocently
around his neck,
he would open every meal
with, *Mommy, what was this
it was alive?*
just as I was picking up
my fork, or when I
poured gravy over
mashed potatoes (as we
did in those days)
he would ask,
Is that blood?

Old Movies

Bingeing TMC, I notice
that women and girls
are always
screaming,
fainting,
throwing themselves
on beds and sobbing
or sitting at vanities
and brushing, brushing
their hair
and remember
how I, as a teen,
tried to imitate that
but never managed
 anything but the hair.

Notes for an Ekphrastic Poem

"What's that you have there?" the man said. "Is that a pen?"

I nodded and held it up, retracting the point with a tiny click

"Sorry, Miss. We don't allow pens in here."

"Really? Where does it say that? I didn't see any signs
about that when I came in."

"It doesn't say, but we don't allow it."

Guilty, I heard. *Guilty of pen, in the first degree.*
Of ink and writing.
Notes. Guilty of notes.

"But what can I do? I'm here
to take notes."

"I can let you have this." He pulled
a pencil stub from his breast pocket–
three inches, a sharp point.

A person *who wanted to*
could do a lot of damage with that.

"But I'll need it back," he added
as I grabbed it, trying to recapture
whatever ideas I had before we met.

He kept his eye right on me after that.

Mending Girls

Something there is that doesn't love a girl.
High school girls still call each other *slut*
and *bitch* in screeching echoes down the halls

buildings meant to be oases, nurturers
builders of self-esteem and self-control,
exemplars of all that's good and right

Welcoming newbies into the fold,
embracing mutual regard and even–
dare we hope–love?

Years later, a female mentor told me,
"Don't publish that. If you do,
they'll call you a slut, for sure."

Pretty Girl

"You're a very pretty girl."
the old professor said—

"a pretty, pretty girl,"
the married old professor said.

But he wasn't Professor Baer
and he wasn't Papa Baer.

It wasn't like that at all.
It wasn't at all like that.

Engraving

Engrave this
on the tablet of your memory,
the old professor said
as he turned
to write on the board
or faced us in his beard
to underscore a point
with a finger.

But what my mind engraved
was the Golden Labrador
asleep beside his desk
and the elbow patches
on his tweed jacket.

Freshman, I was homesick
for the dog I once had–
bought at a shop when I was nine–
a black and tan mutt
I named Daisy
after Dagwood's
when I was still reading something
other than dry pages
from the old professor's book.

Shalimar

Pale hands I love
beside the Shalimar…
my husband sings, waking.
I ask him for the rest
but he stops, unable to
remember, like so much
he can't these days.
Still, I rejoice, because
he's singing, and I know
how lucky I am to have
a man like him—no,
not like him—*him,*
this very man who wakes
each morning with
an old song on his lips.

"If I should die before I wake..."

When his brother died at ninety
my husband said, as he fell asleep,

"I hope Henry remembered to say
his "Now I lay me's."

I pictured two little boys in night-
shirts, their mother standing by.

My mother made me kneel
to say mine.

Bomb

The bombshell came
when he was at work
two hours away
and his daughter called
demanding to speak to Dad–
a request I had to deny
when she screamed to tell me why.
Her sister had killed herself
with a gunshot to the heart
driving the young one mad
and driving us apart.
But if my call would drive him home
I couldn't take that chance.
How could he drive on winding roads
with madness in his ears?
Instead I took upon myself
the job of telling him,
beloved husband, father of two
grown-up women now.
Did he fall apart? Of course he did.
I shouldered all the blame.
The bombshell shattered what he had,
replacing it with shame.

After

Her sister made her bed.
I swept her floor.

We emptied all her cupboards,
shut her door.

The note she left was meant
to tell us more.

But all it said to us was
she was dead.

Privacy

A gun in the car instead of the house.
Did this preserve the home's deep privacy?

What happens when our clumsy thumbs disturb
the surface dust conserving privacy?

How could we assume the right to probe
the pocketbook's reserve, that privacy?

Lipstick, tampon, comb, 1.d,
daybook, cellphone–serving privacy?

A missed appointment her sole plan.
The hole in her heart its solace, privacy.

My name, Irene, is peace; it should be hers.
Solo, only, lonely. Privacy.

Friend

You're not my friend,
a friend who later
killed himself said.
Friends are people
you see every day.

What would he have
thought if he had lived
to see all these
requests to "friend"

people he might
never see?

Is It Ever Too Soon?

To learn about death
as my child did

at two?

I didn't mean
to teach it that way

but that is what
I did

"Don't ever open
that door

with the kitten
in your arms"

I said in my sternest
Mommy voice

and so it happened.

The car…
not fast at all

yet driving past
and my child

had to learn
that way

which must be why
on a recent visit

I was warned,

"If you get a cat
you'll never see

me again."

So now
we have

only dogs
a bowl of goldfish

and a parrot.

To My Father for the Baseball Glove, Long Overdue

When he was twelve, you wrote and asked
for his hand-size so you could send him
a baseball glove. A really good one, you said.

When he was sixteen and away at school, it came:
a glove for the hand of a twelve-year-old
and a package of books for me.

It was a good glove. Your grandson said that
later. Too bad you never met him.
You would have liked each other.

As for the books, I liked those too, although
they were the same as some you sent before.
When She Was Good by Philip Roth

came at least twice. Maybe because
the title was like the rhyme you used to say
whenever I was bad–which was often, I guess.

Remember how you told the story
of "The Boy Who Cried Wolf" when I
called too many times from my crib

for a drink of water? Did you know that
all I wanted was to keep you there?
can't get you back even now.

Nevertheless, I thank you for these messages
sent with care across the great divide:
the baseball glove, the packages of books,

the V-mail letters every week through high school,
their red-white-and-blue borders saying
father, somewhere, love.

Your darling daughter, as in *Yes, my...*
was how I signed my letters then,
and here I am still.

Her Letter

You're no kin of mine, my grandmother wrote,
in the letter sent to me after she died.

*Perhaps you'll think differently when you know
I bought your father from an ad in the paper.*

Kin. Farm-bred, she used that country word.
Bought. What you'd say of a puppy,

what I'd said of mine. Whatever did she mean?
Were babies *bought* in 1899? Perhaps.

Perhaps, perhaps. Later I learned one truth.
Grandpop was really mine, as Daddy was,

but Nana wasn't, never had been.
We shared a name, but that was all.

Genetics had their way; we weren't alike, except
in everything I learned from her, admired:

her cooking, sewing skills, housekeeping,
shopping savvy, structured life, the opposite

of all the messiness at home, disorderly
emotions, angry exits, anxious waits.

I wanted to be like Nana, always did.
My mother sent me there so I could learn.

Found Myself Again. And You?

How do we find ourselves
after losing
and being lost again?

Simple

    music
    music
    more
    more
    more

Bongo

    Banjo
    Dulcimer
    Mandolin

Boom

    Let it do
    its thing

That one

    simple
    thing.

Let sound

　　pour
　　more
　　more.

II

Celebrate!

"Senate Votes to Avert Shutdown"

The stamps I buy say "Celebrate!"

"Default Threat Generates Fear Around Globe"

The stamps I buy say "Celebrate!"

"U.S. Sees Direct Threat in Attack"

The stamps I buy say "Celebrate!"

"Ground Gives Way and a Town Struggles"

The stamps I buy say "Celebrate!"

"What are we celebrating?" I ask.

The postmistress shrugs, counts change.

Each stamp says "Forever" at the top.

Note: All headlines are from *The New York Times*,
     September 2013

Red

Back when I was bold and louder
the postcard, all in red, screamed,
When are you going to introduce
your students to Che Guevara?

Parent or colleague, I didn't know,
but whoever wrote it thought, I guess,
that high school kids shouldn't be told
about the world outside the one

they lived inside and knew so well–
suburban green and false-brick paved–
with school budgets voted every year
so they could be saved from those like me

who had watched Castro on TV.

Responsible

—for my daughter

We spay our dogs because
it's the responsible thing to do;

too many in the world with fleas,
ticks, worms, mange, what-have-you,

festering with sores, neglected, underfed—
but still—I can't help thinking

about that other responsibility,
to the nature that wants one thing:

to reproduce itself—what she, my dog,
would do if she found herself with puppies.

Did these come from me? she might ask,
the way she asks me everything,

watching them wiggle, cuddle, put up
their tiny mouths to nurse, letting them,

feeling good, watching with delight
as they grew and became playmates,

little toys and friends, as I watched you.

Mouse

Curled up as if asleep,
a baby mouse

the comma
of its tail

rigid

its brown fur

a stiff reproach

in my basement.

No crack anywhere.

No toehold.

You left me no recourse,
the tiny body said.

Nothing left to do
but go dead.

Naming the Animals

Who would ever name a dog Audrey
—or Irene?

Has anyone?

But somewhere there must be
a cat named Emily
or Jezebel
a dachshund Anneliese
Weimaraner Anne Marie.

My husband, bless his heart,
always wanted
a basset hound named Maud,

but in case any Mauds
are reading this
I won't go on about
why it made me laugh.

I knew a shrink once
who named his female dog
Oedipus because, he said,
"Things are not always
what they seem."

Have you ever really
known a dog called Rover
or Spot?
A cat named Tabitha?

I haven't, either.

But it occurs to me now
that I'd love to use *Clover*
for a St. Bernard.

Animals Are Disappearing from Our Lives

Had it not been for the zoos
I would not have seen lions, tigers,
great lizards, snakes.
Had it not been for the circus
I would not have put a peanut
in an elephant's mouth.
Had it not been for pet shops,
I would not have had a puppy
nor come home with a cardboard
container of goldfish or a turtle.
Not any of the above, since
most have been deemed
Cruel to Animals
which they most likely are
but, unknowing child that I was,
I would have been without
living, breathing, terrifying,
gorgeous, strokable, huggable,
magnificent ANIMALS.

After Alice

Dolor and doubt
arrived, as expected.
But then we learned
her brother, litter-mate,
had also reached
his expiration date.
Best if used by…
and then…poof!
Like us. Almost.

We didn't consider,
just risked.
And now, Abbie's here,
biting us with little
puppy teeth.
Piddle and poop
are what it's about.
The shades are up.
The sun is out.

The Elephant in the Room

At dinner parties
no one speaks of it
because no one knows,
lifting a fork or spoon,
whether others can see
the massive creature
who stands at the thresh-
old looking on—trunk
curling over the table,
mouth opening wide—
the way the one
at the zoo would always
do for me, shoulder-
hoisted so I could drop
a peanut in, and watch
as it disappeared.

Another One Back

The Tasmanian pademelon
which looks like a dog
and smells like

something to eat
has come back
been sighted

some say

but some say
a lot of things
too many

to get excited about
but not too many

to hope.

Mother's Day

Who would have thought
we'd see a tail?

But there it was, this morning,
sticking out of the Home Defense

trap under the television—
the one that promised

we'd never have to see or touch
the first thing I'd killed

bigger than a fly. I asked
my husband, who pried it open,

what it looked like, dead—
the little creature who'd been

dodging us, darting across the room,
ducking behind a curtain or

a pile of books, the dog not bothering
to bark or even open her eyes.

Apparently, it was a black lump,
with a long tail.

"Tail?" the dog said, alert. "Did I
hear something about a tail?"

Through the window, a gnarl on the oak
looks like the face of Porky Pig.

Mickey's in the trash. New traps await
his brothers–or his mother.

Forgiveness

One banana left in the bowl
its peak of ripeness:
yellow, mottled with brown.

I peel and slice it
for the banana's sake, not mine.

This banana
needs to be eaten.

Is that what W. C. knew
about the plums?

Should he have asked *them*
for forgiveness?

Keeping Our Heads

Was it only me—or did it seem
that just when the papers started
talking about beheadings
everyone, I mean everyone
in America started wearing scarves
folded, wrapped 3x and looped
as if to bandage their necks
against whomever might come
after them with scimitar,
macheté or long knife?
Even in summer, when the
scarves, just as long,
turned gauzy and matched
their outfits?
Was it just me, my worldview,
or yours too?
I mean, Europeans—even men—
always knew how to wrap
a stylish scarf, but you,
my fellow Americans,
when, exactly, did you begin?
Decapitation was too difficult,
the media must have decided—
and besides—*beheading*
has an Ali Baba ring.

Paper Wars

Released time from work–two hours a week
if we would volunteer. Soup Kitchen was mine.
Women with children mostly, too young for school
and the free breakfast that could hold a kid all day.

We made sandwiches, passed them along with paper
bowls of macaroni or potato salad, cups of apple juice
or milk. One mother asked where the napkins were.
Seeing none, I asked the woman-in-charge, who looked

at me as if I had two heads. After a long uncomfortable
minute, she swiped the back of her hand across her mouth
and laughed. "If we gave these people napkins," she said
in a hoarse whisper, "they'd end up on the floor."

2.

Months later, duty took me to city schools
where the powers-that-were had decreed no towels
or even toilet paper in lavatories. Instead, an assistant
told me, children had to go up to a teacher's desk,

say what they wanted to do (shades of Paris metro)
and be handed a couple of pieces from a roll.
Toilet paper, that was. She didn't say aught about
towels, didn't seem to care about filthy hands.

or an eighth-grade girl with her period. Couldn't
get a drink of water, either. All the fountains were
turned off, a supervisor explained patiently,
so that the kids couldn't wad them up with paper.

3.

Fast-forward years to a well-regarded "rehab"
facility, with one wing populated mostly by
indigent elderly in long-term care. To visit
a friend's private room, I had to walk down

a very long corridor, where an old man
hobbled, clinging to a rail, his nose dripping.
He sniffed, but it dripped on his hospital
gown and dribbled where he had already peed.

True to form, I asked in faux naivete
whether someone could give him a tissue.
"We don't give them tissues," the aide said.
"If we did, they'd end up on the floor."

Back to Princeton from Trenton

Why do I think the word
    cyanamid
as I ride this train,
collar gathering grime
and someone behind
singing in my ear?
Across the aisle
muscles move
in and out, in and out
to the jaws' rhythm.

Boxlike houses
running behind windbreak
sing *utility, utility*
to tarpaper shelters
by the railbed.
Amtrak blurs
red-white-blue
as an orange derrick
raises its erection
to the Goodyear sign.

New Brunswick
announces itself
with purple breath.

To Donald Hall

I've heard you read more than once.
I have most of your books, signed.
The last time I saw you I took them
and stood on line to say, "I'll bet you
haven't seen *this* one in a long time;
 would you sign it?" And you said,
"I'll sign all of them," graciously.

And now you've unpacked your boxes
in Grandpa Wesley's house, Jane is gone,
and you say, in *Essays after Eighty,*
that all you can write is prose.

I'm sorry you think your poetry's gone
And you can now govern only in prose.
You did a great job with your new *Selected;*
Your taste hasn't left you at all.

But what I wish you would do for us now
is push open the door, go outside and
kick the leaves again. Bring back
a bright new poem—the poem of a
ninety-year-old, in bloom.

Note: Donald Hall died on June 23, 2018, at 89.

Old Fool

What do they think has happened, the old fools,
To make them like this?

    —Philip Larkin

At night after supper
I sit in my wheelchair
near the elevator
making noises
nobody seems to hear,
diaper slowly filling
as the nurse
gumshoes past,
stethoscope bobbing
on her plump white chest.
I touch myself and drool,
unable to help it
only a little—
more because
the laughing women
at the nurses' station
seem to expect it—
just as they expect
my door to stand open
now that nobody
wants to come in.

Juicy Fruit

The boy on the train—
his seat in front of mine—
was chewing gum
expressively
and talking, talking
seemingly to himself.
Then I saw the head
of a girl beside him,
much lower, listening.
He kept talking, talking.
She kept listening.
When he bent down
to give her a big kiss,
I couldn't help wondering
when I saw the crumpled
package on the floor
if she could taste
his well-chewed
Juicy Fruit.

Reading the News

Is like listening
to a beating drum
or a ticking clock
while trying to stay
asleep.

III

Sub-prime Crisis Hits Women Hard

-Newspaper Headline

I don't know what
came over us–that we did what we did
and ended up
walking home nearly two hundred blocks
from Times Square–too late for supper
and two screaming mothers–except
that we were twelve. To us, from Inwood,
it was "the city," with all its glitz.
So that May Saturday, with a quarter each,
we dropped our nickels in the slot
 and rocketed on basket-weave seats
that made crisscross patterns on our thighs
and left us sweaty and excited
when the doors whooshed open
and my best friend and I
inhaled that subway air
and ran upstairs
to neon blinking in sunlight.
Girls, Girls, Girls, Beer, Beer,
Nedick's, Hot Dogs, Orange Drink.
But we wanted ice cream–
so we bought cones,
and bounced up 42nd
in our saddle shoes and bobby-sox
with one strawberry, one vanilla

double-scoop, sprinkles on each,
went back for more
and looked in all the windows
and up at the marquees
until the sky began to darken
and our money was gone.

Election Snob

Baseball caps, pick-ups,
tattoos, gutturals…
Are these what we're supposed
to love and vote for?

What happened to respect
for education, intellect?
When did poverty lose *genteel*
and shabby its *gentility?*

Why does rising not mean
anything, unless from nothing?
Is denim worthier
than worn-out silk?

I must admit, I miss my ilk.

November 2005

Now, as we move toward
Thanksgiving, U.S.A.,
I read of a baby
who floated face down
in the bathtub where
his mother left him
while she
listened to CD's
in another room.

A couple of months ago
someone's grandmother
floated face down
in a canal of sewage
after the levee broke
and nobody came.

I say this now
to all of us floating
face up
and to all of us sitting
in our chairs
and waiting:

let us try
to keep our own heads
above this
rising water.

Educational Reform

The teacher asleep in his classroom
became the mayor.
He drove us out, took over the system
Is his school any better now—
or worse?

Status quo would be worse,
the law of entropy
(taught to me by a student in '65)—
a law I've observed to work
implacably.

God bless that kid.
I hope he's still alive.

Shooting

Every day there is a shooting.
Every day some fool with a gun

Is shooting some other
fool with a gun

or, helpless without a gun,
wishes he had a gun

so he could shoot, too
because shooting

is what they do.

Note to reader: obviously, this was written before our recent mass
shootings of innocents.

Capitalism: The American Ghazal (Swizzle)

…we're forced to enter the market just to live

–Corey Robin in *The New York Times*

We're forced to enter the market just to live.
My time is up; the battery is dead.

Or maybe a new battery's not all
I'm forced to enter the market for to live.

If I want to set the time, I'll buy a clock
I'm forced to enter the market for to live.

If I buy the clock I can't afford the book
I'm forced to enter the market for to live.

If this is all, what are we living for?
The market will survive, with or without

me as a willing participant–or you,
forced to enter the market just to live.

World News

1

The Nigerian man who has coffee
in my dining-room
as we talk over a sales contract
tells me of his wife and son
and his Igbo patronym, *sacrificer*.
When he tells me of his father
I tell him of my mother.
He kisses my cheek before he leaves.

2

Do you mind if I call you Mother?
the Egyptian cabdriver asks
when he turns to give me change.
 No, I say. But why?
Because you are so kind, he says.
Because you understand.

Norman

for Deborah Solomon

Why do I think of Norman
at the Bates Motel
when I think of poor, tormented
Norman Rockwell?

How dare you? Some would say–
censoring my thoughts
the way they witch-hunt
his biographer.

He was *wholesome–*
and very kind–as if those traits
didn't square
with *gay.*

The kind of gay they want
Is jollity and fun:
the bare-bummed boy
at the doctor's

or the one dressed
in grown-up Sunday best
with nippled bottle sticking
from his breast pocket.

Plunder

Prostitutes were once called *wrens,*
I learn, and a certain type
of Englishman called young women
birds–at least the ones that seemed
available for plunder.

Is *plunderous* a word, I wonder,
like a bird ready for stuffing?
Look it up and find
it's the do-er not the done-to,
as it should be.

And *plunderable*, wouldn't you know,
is there as well.

Reality

"Reality is whatever
we say it is,"
say the masters
as we march to the end
of the bridge.

The Land Speaks

I was Earth. I was Gaia.
My fields were green, lush,
my leaves and fruits abundant.
In my trees, birds sang
who now are silent.
Was it you who did this?
I am cracked and gray.
Great crevices open
where I have dried.
Seeds are cast but lie
on my surface only.
Nothing will sprout or flower.
The bees are dying.
Bats lie dead outside their caves,
white-nosed with fungus.
I can no longer revive or shelter
my creatures, my children.
I am broken. If you are walking
on my skin, I cannot
feel or hear you.

IV

The Great American Novel

He would not look behind his father's saying....
       –Robert Frost

There was the man who kept on working
until he was ninety-six, who said:

In my family we don't decline; we just
drop dead, which he did

and the woman who kept a lover for twenty years
while sleeping beside a husband and washing socks

because in her family they didn't split
and so she didn't

and kept on voting the same Party every year
without reading the news

because in her family that was what they did
and what they said

and the woman who kept on writing poems
because her sixth-grade teacher had said:

"Someday you'll write
The Great American Novel."

But her mother kept saying:
"I love your poems."

Her Fragments

I have no pictures of you as a little girl.
What did you look like?

St. Marks Place…
My mother made my clothes.
A little white dog named Peggy.

Why no pictures, Mother?

I saved Peggy in the fire.

What fire?

There was a fire.

What fire? Tell me.

I was on fire.
They wrapped me in a blanket
to put out the flames…

I was on fire.

My Mother at Sixty

Loved to remind me she was old.
"We seniors," she would say, "We seniors,"
as she tied on her heavy shoes, picked up
her cane. Mistress of demographics, she'd ask
what I thought of "these teen-agers,"
as if a band of zombies or Martians
had invaded the streets of her beloved city
the only place that wasn't
"in the middle of nowhere,"
meaning not New York.
Here it was she could practice
her brand of thrift:
extra packets of Equal
from the bowl at the Senior Center
bank deposit slips
to use for note paper–all
went into her giant pocketbook,
repository of pay stubs,
Chiclets, roll after roll
of Tums and secrets.

Her Smile

She smiles. She has always smiled.
Now my mother smiles because she is eighty-one.
Because she has so little hair.
Because the teeth she bought at fifty are even and white.
Because her feet and knees hurt and she needs the cane
she bought when she was seventy-five.
Because if they like her smile they may touch her
and she wants so much to be touched
that she smiles when the doorman places a hand
on her back as he holds open the door of the car
or the girl in the beauty shop picks up a brush
and lays it gently against her scalp
or my dog noses her skirt, jumps on her lap
and gives a low, pleasured growl.
The mailman puts stamps in her hand and she smiles
as his fingers touch her palm, asks for change
so she can feel his fingers again.
At home, she lifts the doll's dress,
strokes its hard buttocks through the ruffled drawers,
squeezes the bear before she lays it on the bed.

My Mother at 85

Disappearing into age,
she forgets
my husband's name
her own size
and where
the new nightgowns
I brought her in the nursing-home
have gone. Selectively,
as birds do, she builds nests
of salvage: the other afghan,
cotton wool, Vaseline.

"There, in the middle drawer
of the dresser, to the right,"
she directs from her metal bed,
the left-behind apartment
intact on her memory screen.

Here, in the too-white room,
she summons red: velour robe,
hairbrush, neck pillow, scarf–

and me, the mouse she clicks
to call up virtual reality.

Coming to Live with Me

The middle of nowhere
was what she called
wherever I lived
after I left New York.

Where are all the people?
she would say
as she parted a blind
or pulled open a drape.

Oh, look–a dog walked by!
she said one cold November day
from our sunporch,
rubbing it in.

This house is too big
was what it came down to
after the last of her things
were gone, the apartment cleared

of even the black dial telephone
she hadn't wanted to give up
and her *valise,* as she called it,
lay on the bed in our guestroom.

It was two steps up to the living-room,
but she called it *going upstairs*–
as if from one room to another
were a journey, like going to work
on the subway, with stairs
to the street level, with people
pushing from behind and at your side
and dogs busy on leashes at curbs.

When I left for work each morning
she was forlorn till I returned.
Lonesome, she called it. *Lonesome*
like a howl or a cowboy moan.

A companion? Where would she sleep?
At the foot of my bed, my mother said,
opening her mind's valise
to let me in.

After She Died

I woke up angry
at my mother in a green coat
wrinkled from the bag she'd
stowed it in
and stained at the hem.

I wanted to cry

but the wrinkles and stains
enraged me so
I couldn't
sleep again that night
until I knew:

She led me out of that dark place;
I'll lead her home.

Intact

Perhaps
Not giving up
one's secrets
is a form
of chastity.

Remembering Her Life

There was the man
who wanted to play her again
like an old record
read her again
like a well-remembered book.

She couldn't say that she blamed him
or that she was offended.
Flattered, rather—
appropriately adorned
with the wreath of memory,
the laurel of desire.

Breaking the Line

Some line breaks have
eluded me for years—

as in leaving, you

with duffel packed
in that Maine cottage

I still see, but not
where the line should

break—only where

it did.

Discovery

Conversation with a woman, he said,
as if he'd never had it,

while I, whose words ran through me
like a sieve,

lay there astonished that I had
so much to give

I'd never withheld, and now
this sudden wealth

had found me, as it were,
by stealth–

quite literally in the night
as pastorally

he counseled, complimented
what I little knew

had been my strongest suit:
not beauty, charm,

grace, or even strength of will
but simply talk–

the give-and-take of dialogue
with a man.

Outclassed

Digging into the archive
reading old letters, drafts
I realize that each year
when I look back at her,
the old me was smarter
than I am now.

Unearthed metaphors
gleam, similes sound
as if never heard before.
How clever, sharp-edged, clear
and better than I, poor reader,
can ever hope to be.

I can't compete with her–
nor should I try.

Who Was I?

A girl. A human. That
was all I really knew.
But there in my New York
Manhattan was a country,
the block, a province.
In the street outside
the population
of the under-five-feet
would congregate,
would mill.
One had a ball,
another a rope,
someone else
a piece of chalk.
We'd jump and throw;
We'd scrawl.
Admirers of expertise,
we had our specialties:
Potsy Champ, Jumper
of Double Dutch.
Mine was Funny Stories.
In each new neighborhood
I learned again: make them
laugh or listen
and I was in.

Who Am I?

I carry my father inside
as he must have carried me
until his seed burst forth
in wild ejaculate
to populate her womb–
yet I'm still trying
to learn who I am.

Mirror

Is this what age does?
I don't look old, I think—
just worried and tired,
like the old actors on TV
who look as if they're
about to cry.

Is This It?

Perhaps I'm just
One page
Of an unfinished
Book.

Not Living

I'm not *living* my life,
my old friend said;

I'm *remembering*
my life. I can't

give away my LP's.

V

Retiree

What *am* I now
that we refer to ourselves

by what we used to be?

Hey, what?

I'm still here–
but is it *me?*

Lunch

Yesterday
I went to lunch with two friends
and came back with three thoughts:

1) I'm glad I did my traveling
   when I was young.

2) I still prefer Hemschemeyer's
   translations of Akhamatova.

3) I need solitude more than I need
   a good lunch.

Without

One by one my old friends are leaving.
Who will be left to tell when I go?

Who will do the necessary grieving—
or isn't it essential, after all?

At 90

The world
is running
away from me
like a big balloon
and I'm trying
to hold on to
its string.

90 Plus

This body
is a new body
one I don't yet know
and so—
I must treat it
with respect.

Home Comfort

I take such pleasure from this right-sized plate
and coffee mug of indigo, I wonder

why my toasted bread must lie just so,
jam and butter spread to perfect thickness,

papers picked up slowly at the door–
unfolded to the weather I ignore for crossword puzzles.

Still, this modest happiness is a gift–
breaking fast slowly my favorite

not just meal, but *time*–the hour's quiet
like a down-filled quilt.

A Good Day

Any day when
I write a poem
Before breakfast
Reminds me
Of what makes
A good day.

After Leaving Rehab

Your old body is a new body, so
you have to treat it with respect,
like someone you don't know—yet
and if you're careful enough,
 a new friend.

They Died Laughing

"Laugh? I thought I'd die," we used to say.

But they did, as I recall.

My husband chuckled as he told me how
the fall he didn't know would be his last
 had happened.

My good friend laughed as she said
hospice, hospice, because she thought
I'd been trying to say the name
of a new medicine.

And my brother on the gurney reminded me
of how I'd thought cigarettes were what gave him
cancer and the brain tumor that helped
the doctors find it.

Ha ha, he said. *Ha ha,* I answered back
as we rolled down the corridor together.

How It Is

With grief this great
you can't think
metaphorically.
You can only say
what *is*.

How Are You?

"Dying happily," he said
from his hospice bed,
but truthfully–
the people here
are all so kind, I'd
really rather stay.

Insurers overheard,
evicted as he rallied.
Transferred to
Neglectful Care,
he's leaving anyway,
but sent us word:

"If only more of us
were cosseted, not
buffeted, perhaps
we'd spend more time
not dying."

Chrysalis

Waiting now, for something
that doesn't yet
exist.

Is it for me
to emerge
from this–

the hand
my life
has become

in the cards?
Elsewhere?

Nearly There

Don't write about poems
the masters say—

but how can I not
about the one that got away?

Shopping List

I open my handbag
and another
shopping list
falls out.

Since I stopped driving
I feel as if I'm living
inside a giant
shopping bag.

How Will I Do It?

I have to think it through
as I do most everything, don't I?
Haven't I, all these years
in spite of, because of, without?
Nevertheless.....

Mid-September

Winter began last night.

Pathetic fallacy, my old
professor friend would say,

yet I wake at four
remembering
to the sound of rain
his service is today.

It's raining harder now
—and cold.

We raised a glass
to him the other night.

First time he wasn't there.

Almost Christmas

and the weather here's
miasmic

good for shopping
movies
Chinese food
and books

the kind of thing
the well-prepared
can do

but not me

and perhaps not you.

Last-minute checks,
back-dated
might suffice.

Not as much
as a carefully-wrapped
surprise

but still–

appreciated, I suppose,
by some

who think them just
as good
or better than.

Tell Me a Story

I'll tell you a story
of Jack-a-Nory
and now my story's begun.

I'll tell you another
about his brother
and now my story is done.

So it went
to our pleading
most nights

but every so often
my father would relent
and give us each
what we wanted–
one for my brother
with pirates
and one for me
with a girl, a boy, a dog:
Dolly, Bobby and Comfy.

I can't remember
my brother's story.
Perhaps I wasn't
meant to.

Banished

Whoop, whoop, cough, cough–I've got
the whooping cough! my little brother laughed
as he ran around the playground after school.

Mothers grabbed their children and fled,
but not before one shouted back at *me,*
I'm calling the Board of Health!

Eight years old, reluctantly obedient,
I had brought him only because my mother,
wanting the afternoon off, had told me to.

My brother was four and had heard someone
say the words he found–as he did with so many–
not just funny, but *screamingly* so.

The matron emerged from her hiding-booth
and ordered us out, yelling that I should be
ashamed, not listening as I tried to explain.

Days later, I sneaked in again, to push myself
on the big swings, climb the monkey bars alone–
and try to get someone–*anyone*–to seesaw.

Trinity

One of everything
but a trio in my mind:
the three I pass singly,
heads down in their roles.

The homeless man, our only
(yes, only), reeking always
in the same clothes, though
he owns a house, I'm told.

The Bard, so christened
because he once taught poetry
at the school, long gone,
where our house now stands.

And the long-haired old woman
with the kindly face and
solicitous air of a social worker
is our town's sole prostitute.

Whenever I see them now
I want to say, "Don't give up,"
or leave," and I think how lucky I am
to live in a place like this,

with only one of each.

VI

Tomfoolery

Some Words for Windows

Sit there like a smiling dog,
obedience-trained, leash in mouth,
array of icons like a row of teeth.
Do you, do you, do you?
Yes, I really, really do.
Are you, are you sure?
Yes, yes, yes.
Do you want to shut me off?
I want, I want…
to save whatever I've put in you
and shut you up, up, up
like a vault,
like a god-damned vault.
But are you sure?
Are you really sure?
Why don't you let me
show you my array again
just to be sure?
I don't want to see.
I don't want–
Here it is, anyway.
See how pretty!
All their names
all their tiny names
the ones I've given them
the ones you've given them

the foolish and the brave
the rough drafts and revised.
There's no such thing as a thought
I can't preserve
t h o u g h t . . .
Now it's time to say bye-bye,
o masterful one
o desk genie, wizard
of iconography and sign,
turn off your bells and whistles,
sing * me * home *

Speak!

My dog says.
She's my owner
although I own 'er.
As she climbs on my lap
and stares straight ahead
like a Sphinx,
I wonder what
she thinx.

Visitor

Well, whaddya know?
Shreds of snow

and a big fat squirrel
on my patio–

back against the cushion
of the wicker chair.

If he had arms
they'd be outspread.

Welcome, I say
to this new visitor–

serene in his
entitlement.

Jelly

So familiar
we call it by its nickname,
redolent of lunch-box,
plastic wrap.

So comfortable
in the sound and in the mouth–
(that cool, delicious slide)
that a woman, reading *jelly*

on a tube of contraceptive,
spread it on her toast.

Another Little Ad

Cheery antique mirror
with 2' boarder.

No wonder the mirror is cheery;
Solo, he must've been lonely.

But, as for his tiny boarder–
How did *she* get in?

Or, better still, how–if ever–
will she get out?

The Talking Bookcase

"Antique bookcase. Eloquent."

I wonder, is it also loquacious?
What can you do with a
bookcase that never shuts up?
No wonder you want to get rid of it!

Thanksgiving

She smokes, she drinks, she has a rose tattoo.
Her mother tries to bite her tongue but doesn't.
They fight, they scream, the daughter hightails out,
grabs the car and zooms. Cops are called.
Assault is charged by someone; handcuffs now,
headlines tomorrow, mug shots, fingerprints.
Another blast, household a disaster–
turkey on the floor and stuffing splattered.
The dog laps up the mess and belches loudly.
Auntie laughs and has another drink.
Mom's in bed with a migraine; Sis in the clink.

Pursuit

A friend writes
that she's going to *pursue*
graduate studies.

An interesting assertion
since we don't send
our children off

to *pursue* school;
they just get on the bus
or take our hands, and *go*.

What is all this
about an M.A. or Ph.D.
that makes it seem

so hard to catch?

The Past

The past is really gaseous
It almost makes me nauseous
To think of just how gaseous it is.

But when you're feeling nauseous
It's best to avoid the gaseous.
Surely you must agree.

I know this conversation
Does not yield much elation
And little to relieve anxiety,

And so will resume quietude
Out of my solicitude
For you–but even more, for me.

Gizmo

Today I got a message
that used the word *gizmo*.
What a wonderful word!
It makes me want to sing it,
say it—again and again.
All together now: Gizmo!
Louder: Gizmo, Gizmo, Gizmo!!!

About the Author

Irene Willis has published five previous poetry collections, plus an anthology of poems called *Climate of Opinion: Sigmund Freud in Poetry* (IPBooks, 2017) and another, co-edited with Jim Haba, called *What They Bring: The Poetry of Migration and Immigration* (IPBooks, 2020).

Three times nominated for Pushcart Prizes and once for a National Book Award, her poems have also appeared in many journals and anthologies. She has received a Distinguished Artist Award from the New Jersey State Council on the Arts, a residency fellowship from the Millay Colony for the Arts, and a grant from the Berkshire/Taconic Foundation.

She attended St. Lawrence University, holds a B.S. from SUNY Fredonia, an M.A. and Ph.D. from New York University, and a M.F.A. in Poetry from New England College.

A longtime educator who has "retired" three times, she has taught in high schools, colleges and graduate schools, most recently at Westfield State University and American International College, both in Massachusetts.

An Emeritus member of the Authors' Guild, she is Poetry Editor of www.internationalpsychoanalysis.net, where she has a monthly column called "Poetry Monday."

Acknowledgments

As always, I would like to thank Olivia VanSant, P.A. *extraordinaire,* my beloved Springer Spaniel, Abigail, who is somehow always with us, in spirit or as herself, when we work with anything connected with poems.

I am forever grateful for the supportive fellowship of Lisken Van Pelt Dus, Cynthia Gardner, Hilary Russell, Phil Timpane, our U.K. member, Chris Fogg, and my morning poetry buddy, David Giannini.

Much gratitude also to Arnold Richards, M.D., a poet himself, and to Tamar and Larry Schwartz of IPBooks, for being there and for doing whatever needs to be done, whenever.